CHURCH OF THE NAZARENE

DATE DUE

DEMCO 38-297

The Forbidden Tunnel

by
Bruce Nuffer
and
Brittany Browning

Beacon Hill Press of Kansas City
Kansas City, Missouri

Copyright 1997
by Beacon Hill Press of Kansas City
Printed in the
United States of America

ISBN 083-411-6502

Editor: Micah W. Moseley

Illustrations by Jim Seward

Unless otherwise indicated, all Scripture quotations are taken from the *Holy Bible, New International Version*® (NIV®). Copyright © 1973, 1978, 1984 by International Bible Society. Used by permission of Zondervan Publishing House. All rights reserved.

Quotations from the *New Revised Standard Version* (NRSV) of the Bible, copyright 1989 by the Division of Christian Education of the National Council of the Churches of Christ in the USA. Used by permission. All rights reserved.

Note: This book is part of the Understanding Christian Mission, Children's Mission Education curriculum. It is designed for use in Year 2, The Bible in Mission. This study year examines the importance of the Bible in the mission enterprise. This book was chosen for use in this year because it gives children insights into the importance of the Bible to missionaries as well as the unsaved. This book was based on the life experience of Brittany Browning, MK in the Holy Lands.

10 9 8 7 6 5 4 3 2 1

This book was written in the fall of 1995. In September 1996, rioting broke out in Jerusalem in the immediate area around the Dome of the Rock. The fury of the Palestinians and Israelis concerned excavations in a certain tunnel running under the Temple Mount. Truth is indeed stranger than fiction.

Chapter One

"Oomph! Gasp! Aargh!" Andrew struggled against his captor.

"Don't turn around!" growled a voice in Andrew's ear. A strong hand covered his mouth. Andrew was silent.

Andrew's parents had warned him that Old Jerusalem could be dangerous. It just wasn't as safe as the modern city of Jerusalem that surrounded it. But he never thought anyone would want to hurt him.

"I'm a missionary!" Andrew tried to yell. But the sound came out muffled. Then Andrew remembered a verse. "'Do not fear, for I am with you,'" he said to himself. Andrew had learned that verse during the Persian Gulf War. His family had left Jerusalem for safety. Andrew remembered it whenever he was afraid.

As he calmed down, Andrew noticed his friend, Yoni (YO-nee) Katz. Yoni had a big smile on his face. Andrew shoved the hand off his mouth and spun around. Yoni burst out laughing. George Abu-Hannah stood behind Andrew, smiling. He was Andrew's friend from school.

"Ha! I scared you to death!" laughed George.

Andrew stared at his friends. Then he burst out laughing. He was glad it was a joke. His heart was beating hard.

"What are you guys doing here?" George asked. He was surprised to see them in the market.

"Yoni found a coin on the beach at Caesarea the other day. It looks pretty old," said Andrew. "We want to find a coin dealer. Maybe he'll know if it's worth anything."

"Let's see it," George said to Yoni.

Yoni pulled the object from his pocket. Strange markings covered it.

"Weird," said George quietly, studying the coin. "This looks pretty old. Hey, I know where we can find an antique dealer! It's only a couple blocks from here."

Yoni looked frightened. "You won't mind if I wait here, will you?" His shoulders drooped as he looked straight at George. Yoni was pretty short and thin. His friends called him Bones. When he stood straight, Andrew thought he looked like a board.

Yoni was Jewish. George had pointed to the Palestinian part of the city. Old Jerusalem is split into several areas. Jews live in one of the areas. Palestinians live in another. The two groups don't like each other very much. Yoni was scared to go into the Palestinian part of town.

"Come on, Bones. You'll be OK because you're with me," said George. George was Palestinian, and some of his relatives lived in Old Jerusalem. Yoni and George were good friends despite their different cultures.

"He's right," said Andrew. "Come with us."

"OK." Yoni gave in. He was a kid. He doubted anyone would pick on him after all.

"Great!" Andrew cheered. "Let me ask my dad if I can go." He ran past several merchants selling bread and fruit. He found his dad buying spice from an old woman sitting in a doorway.

"Be back here in exactly one hour," Mr. Anderson said when Andrew asked if he could go with his friends. As Andrew ran back to Yoni and George, his father yelled after him, "And don't go looking for trouble!"

George led Andrew and Yoni down narrow alleys and crowded streets. People scurried in and out of doorways. One alley was so narrow that Andrew almost tripped over two men playing *shesh-besh* (backgammon).

The boys finally walked through another alley and out onto a wide street.

"It's right over there." George pointed across the street toward the open antique shop.

Behind the counter stood a man reading a newspaper. He wore a tall fez (Turkish hat) and sunglasses. The man picked his long yellow teeth with a letter opener. He was not much older than Andrew's dad. However, his skin looked tough, like leather. Even though he looked the same as other store owners, Andrew was afraid of him. The boys walked up to the counter.

"Do you know anything about coins?" asked George.

"Of course," the man said. His voice crackled. Andrew wondered if he was telling the truth. Maybe he was just pretending because they were kids.

"Well, is this worth anything?" asked Yoni. He held out his coin for the man to see.

Picking it up, the man looked at it closely.

"Let's see," he mumbled.

The boys stood quietly, waiting for the man's response.

"Hmmm," the shopkeeper said softly. He rubbed

the coin with his thumb. He studied the strange markings for a long time. He turned the coin over and over. The boys grew anxious.

Andrew reached for the coin in the man's hand. The shopkeeper snatched it away before Andrew could grab it. "I must look at it very closely!" the man scolded Andrew.

Andrew drew back in disgust. He thought the man might actually keep the coin. The man softly laughed to himself. The boys didn't think there was anything funny. Slowly the man reached under the counter. He took out a book and quickly turned the pages. He stopped turning and read. Then he studied the coin and read some more. The boys looked at each other. Wham! The man slammed his book.

"Where did you find this?"

Chapter Two

The boys jumped away from the counter. They were ready to run out the door.

The man realized he had scared the boys. He apologized.

"I'm sorry to be so jumpy." He looked at the coin for another moment. "I recently found a piece that looks like this. It would be very odd for us to find matching pieces."

"Is it a valuable coin?" George asked.

"Not really," the man answered.

The man could tell the boys didn't believe him, so he explained.

"At first I thought you had found a seal—a sign of someone important."

Andrew piped up, "I want to find something really big—something really important."

"Ha!" the man laughed. "Then you are on a search for Noah's ark."

"What?" asked Yoni.

"You are looking for things you will never find." The old man laughed. Andrew's face turned red.

"Hey, we're going to find something so important . . . ," Yoni blurted out. The other boys looked at him in amazement.

"Then maybe you want to look for seals and rings. Kings used their signet rings to make the seals," the man said, handing the coin back to Yoni. "I thought you had found a seal. But it is not. Both are very rare. Few have been found."

The boys asked a lot of questions. Andrew was so interested that he almost forgot about meeting his dad. "Come on, Yoni," he said, as he tugged on his friend's arm. "My dad's waiting on me."

Andrew, Yoni, and George were excited. They talked about rings and seals all the way back to Andrew's dad. They wanted to find a signet ring.

"We'd be famous," said George.

"Think how important a ring like that would be," Yoni remarked.

"We'd go down in history like that shepherd boy who found the Dead Sea Scrolls," added Andrew excitedly. Andrew always wanted to find something important.

"Hey, let's come back tomorrow," said George. "Maybe that man can tell us where we should start looking."

"Yeah," said Yoni. "I don't like hanging around that part of town, but I agree with George. We need to talk to that man some more. I'm not even sure what a signet ring is."

* * *

In Old Jerusalem the next day, the boys returned to the antique dealer's store. Yoni grabbed the handle and pulled. The door wouldn't budge. It was locked. Andrew peered through the window. The room was dark and quiet.

"It's closed," said Andrew.

"Aw, man!" George complained. "Now what are we gonna do?"

"Oh, come on, guys. There's got to be another

place around here where we can find some help," insisted Yoni.

The boys walked for several blocks. They passed rows and rows of people selling food and trinkets. After a while, George slowed down. He stopped at a table and pretended to look at what the merchant was selling.

"What are you doing?" Andrew asked. "I thought we were looking for a coin shop."

"My mom needs some spice," George said. The other two were not convinced. George looked worried.

"There's got to be another store nearby. Maybe in another block or two," said Andrew.

When he said that, a funny thought struck Yoni. "George doesn't want to go to the Jewish quarter," he said.

It was true. The boys were leaving the Palestinian part of the Old City. They were headed to the Jewish part.

"You've got to be kidding!" Andrew said, frustrated. "What is it with you two?"

Yoni and George both looked at Andrew. Andrew knew there was no reason for Yoni and George to fear each other. Yoni was a Jew. George was a Muslim (MUZ-lem). So what? Andrew didn't understand.

"Look," George began, "you can't understand what it's like for Yoni and me. Our people don't like each other. Yoni and I are best friends. But that doesn't mean all Jews will like me."

"But the Bible says, 'Love one another,'" Andrew argued. "Jesus Christ wasn't an enemy to anyone."

"Hmmph," Yoni mumbled.

Andrew knew a little about the Jewish religion. He

knew that the Jews do not believe Jesus is God's Son. It was hard talking about Jesus to Yoni. Yoni was still waiting for Christ to come to the earth the first time.

George was a little easier to talk to. Because his religion was Islam, he, too, believed there was a person called Jesus. Yet George thought Jesus was just a prophet, like Abraham or Moses.

Andrew kept trying. "The Bible says to honor one another above yourselves."

"Not my Bible," said Yoni. "The Jewish religion does not follow Christ's commands in the New Testament. We follow the laws found in the Torah. The Torah is the first five books of the Old Testament."

"Jesus was a great man," George told Andrew, "but you give Him too much credit."

George always called God Allah. Andrew was never sure if it was the same as the God he knew. He usually acted as if it was.

Andrew chewed on his lip. He didn't know what to say. He knew Jesus was more than a prophet. He knew He is God's Son. And Andrew didn't think Muhammad was a prophet of God either. But there was just no convincing George of that.

"Let's go," Yoni said, as he continued walking. "I went into your part of town. You can come into mine," he said to George.

The boys didn't have to walk very far before they saw a sign hanging above a door. It read, "Pottery, Coins, Jewelry."

"Maybe someone here can help us," said Yoni.

Inside the store, an old man sat writing at a table. Andrew knew he was a Jew by the *kepa* (KEE-puh: a hat worn by Jewish men) he wore. Bright white hair poked out of it. His eyes squinted as he wrote. Andrew looked around for a cane or staff but didn't see one.

"Ask him if he speaks English," Andrew whispered to Yoni.

"Yes," answered the man, hearing Andrew. "English."

"We're looking for a ring," Yoni volunteered. "A signet ring." He showed him his coin.

"Yeah," said Andrew, "one that makes a seal. Like this one. Well, this isn't really one but almost. We want to find a king's ring or something. Do you know where to look?"

"Ah, you are looking for the rings," the old man repeated. He scratched his long nose with a cracked, gray fingernail. Then he pointed into the air near George.

"Long, long ago," the man began, then stopped. His eyes stared past the boys in deep thought. "Long before you can even imagine, empires swept across this sacred land. These empires took turns ruling. Many wars were fought, and Jerusalem was destroyed 17 times." He held up three fingers. The boys chuckled and nodded. "Each time by a different conqueror.

"First the Assyrians, then the Babylonians. After them, the Persians, Turks, and Crusaders took their turns here. From all ends of the earth they came. Each empire took people and possessions from this land back to its country. And you think the struggle for Jerusalem is only between Arabs and Jews?" The man looked at George and Yoni. "No, no, my friends. People have been fighting for this land forever."

The boys were silent, imagining all the battles that happened in Jerusalem. Finally George spoke up, "So what about the rings?"

"Yes, the rings," the old man remembered. "It is said that in ancient days wealthy men and kings had signet rings to make seals. A picture or word was cut onto a signet ring. The ring was usually iron or stone. Then the ring was pressed onto a piece of wet clay, molten lead, or a quick-drying material. When the ring was removed, an imprint of it was made. It was like writing your name.

"A few rings and seals have been found. I cannot remember whose. I must look in my books. This, what you have, looks like one, but it is only a coin."

"But—but—" Andrew tried to talk.

The man held up his hand to silence him. "The seals and rings of most kings, like David and Solomon, have never been found. I do not believe they ever will be."

"Why not?" asked Yoni.

"For years men have searched for such an important discovery. Finding a seal or the ring of the great King David would make you famous. He was the most important king in history. So many experts have tried and found nothing."

"So how do you know they exist?" Andrew asked.

"Men have looked for so long. Stories have been passed down through the ages. My father's father told me. They must lie in David's city somewhere. King David was too important not to have owned such a ring. Now you boys go home. I have another customer."

Chapter Three

Back in Andrew's living room, the boys talked excitedly about finding a signet ring.

"Outside the wall of the Old City is where King David lived," said Yoni. "We could start looking there."

"I have an old army shovel of my dad's," Andrew added, as his dad entered the room. "It bends in half and is really small. We could carry that with us in case we need to do some digging."

"What about me?" Andrew's father asked, hearing his name mentioned.

"I said I still have that old army shovel you gave me."

"Doing some digging?" asked Andrew's father.

"Only if we have to. We want to find King David's signet ring!" said Andrew. But his dad didn't think it was a very good idea.

"What makes you think it even exists?"

"A man in Old Jerusalem said it exists," Yoni added. "We went to his coin shop. He told us all about it."

"I don't know," Andrew's dad said. "I've done a lot of studying about the historical items around here. But I've never read about King David's signet ring. You feeling a bit like Indiana Jones, or what?"

"Nah, Dad," Andrew said. "This is for real."

"Sure it is," said Andrew's dad, as he left the room.

* * *

After George and Yoni went home, Andrew thought about the discussion he had earlier that day with his friends. He didn't understand how George could think Jesus was only a prophet. And he didn't know how to get Yoni to believe Jesus was God's Son.

"Dad," Andrew finally asked, "why don't Jews believe in Jesus?"

"Some do," Mr. Anderson answered. "Do you mean Jews like Yoni?"

"Yeah."

"That's a hard question. I suppose he doesn't believe in Jesus because his family never has."

"I don't understand. You mean he never will?"

"Never is a long time," Mr. Anderson said. "In Jesus' time, many people thought He was just a prophet or a crazy man. Some thought He was evil because He challenged their religious beliefs. Even after He rose from the grave, many didn't believe He was the Messiah."

"Messiah?"

"It means 'The Promised One.'"

"Oh. How could they deny He was God's Son when He performed so many miracles?"

Mr. Anderson didn't say anything for a second. Then he finally said, "Remember when you were getting notes from a secret admirer at school?"

"Yeah." Andrew turned red. Peggy Davis was the admirer. He had hoped it was Angela Fisher. Peggy was two years younger than him. He had been embarrassed when he found out. He was still embarrassed just thinking about it.

"Who was it you thought was giving you those

notes?" asked Mr. Anderson.

"Angela Fisher," Andrew mumbled, digging his toe into the carpet.

"What does Angela look like?" Mr. Anderson prodded.

Andrew didn't know why his dad suddenly wanted to know, but he answered anyway. "She has long black hair, with big curls. She is a little shorter than me, and she is really smart."

"And how old was the girl who really gave you those notes?"

"She was 9 years old," Andrew replied. He considered it insulting. He was almost 12. But a 9-year-old liked him!

"She wasn't quite what you were expecting, was she?"

"No," Andrew laughed, finding it funny the more he thought about it.

"Well," said Mr. Anderson, "that's sort of how it was with Jesus. Some people wouldn't believe in Him. They always pictured someone different."

"What did they think He would be like?" asked Andrew.

"They always pictured the Promised One being like other kings on earth. They thought He would be big and forceful. They thought He would command armies. But Jesus wasn't like that at all. He looked like an ordinary person. He was a carpenter. He wasn't popular, and He didn't care what people thought of Him. Many people just couldn't believe that the Promised One would look like everyone else or act as He did."

"And today Jews still think this?"

"Well, some Jews think Jesus was a rabbi (a Jewish teacher). But when He was on earth, some Jews believed in Him. People called those that did 'Christians' because they followed Christ."

"Didn't people change their minds when Jesus was raised from the dead?" asked Andrew.

"Some did. But many Jews didn't believe He was ever raised. They said Jesus' followers made up that story. Some Jews, like Yoni, still believe that today."

"So there are many Jews still waiting for the Promised One to come to earth? Yet Christians say He was already here?" asked Andrew.

"That's right."

"So how can I get Yoni to believe in Jesus?"

"You can't," said Mr. Anderson flatly.

"What!" Andrew gasped. "You mean it's impossible?"

"No. But you can't get Yoni to believe anything. God can try to change Yoni's mind. But Yoni must decide for himself what he believes. It might help if Yoni sees that you live a life like Jesus did. He may notice you are different from other kids because you are following Christ's example."

"Then he can be a Christian?"

"When he believes Jesus is God's Son, he can."

"How will I know when he does?"

"You may never know. Only God knows what is in a person's heart. Yoni may begin saying he believes in Jesus to get you to stop bothering him. But God will know when Yoni has really changed. Your job is to love him and pray for him."

❋ ❋ ❋

That evening as Andrew went to sleep, he thought again about his friends. He didn't understand why the Arabs and Jews disliked each other. Sure, he remembered some fights between the two groups. But he never thought it was because they were different culturally.

Andrew's eyes grew heavy. But he couldn't quit thinking of George and Yoni. A year ago there had been a lot of fighting in a city near Jerusalem. Jews and Arabs and even some Christians shot each other and killed many people. Andrew never understood how people could call themselves Christians, yet kill others for no reason. The thought of Yoni and George fighting made him shiver. He had seen men fighting on the news. He wondered . . .

Gunshots! Andrew sat up quickly and listened. Yes! There was definitely gunfire outside! He ran to the living room, where he could see the street from a window. Outside, people of all ages fought with each other. Some people with torches set the cars parked outside on fire. The fire that engulfed his dad's car flickered light on his face. He hid behind the curtains and watched a man with a broom handle fighting off three others.

"God, make these people stop fighting," Andrew prayed. He heard more gunshots from somewhere in the crowd. When he looked back at his father's burning car, he saw two men walking up to his front door. What were they going to do?

Then somewhere a long way off, Andrew heard his name. He looked around but didn't see anyone.

Someone pounded on the door.

"Open up!" a voice said.

"We'll break your door down if you don't open it!" said another.

"NOOOO!" Andrew screamed.

Chapter Four

"Andrew. Honey." Andrew's mother shook him gently, trying to wake him. "Andrew, it's time to get ready for school."

Andrew woke up quickly. His heart raced. Beads of sweat had formed on his forehead. His mother saw the fearful look on his face.

"What's wrong, Andrew?"

"Whew!" Andrew relaxed. "I had a horrible dream."

❋ ❋ ❋

At school that day, Andrew and his friends talked more about where to find a ring. During history, Andrew daydreamed about being a famous explorer. The more he thought about finding a ring, the worse he wanted to start looking. He scribbled a short note to George, "Let's find a ring!"

Andrew slipped the note to the girl next to him and motioned for her to give it to George. As George was reading the note, Andrew heard his teacher announce, ". . . so I want all your parents to sign these permission forms for our field trip to the City of David tomorrow."

Andrew's eyes opened wide. He looked at George.

"Psst!" Yoni whispered, getting Andrew's attention from George. "The City of David! Maybe while we are there, we can find out where to look for a ring!"

George and Andrew were thinking exactly the same thing.

✳ ✳ ✳

The next day a school bus drove slowly along the bumpy roads just outside the wall of Old Jerusalem. George, Yoni, and Andrew sat together.

"George," said Andrew, who was sitting by the window, "do you think this is the place?"

"I don't know," George said.

"I don't know either," added Yoni. "I asked my dad what the City of David was. He said sometimes it means all of Jerusalem."

"All of Jerusalem?" asked Andrew. "We'll never find anything!"

"My dad also said the City of David sometimes means this area of ruins we are going to."

After riding for what seemed like hours, the bus finally stopped. The boys and their classmates piled out of the bus. They found themselves standing on a sloping hill. Trees grew above the boys, up the hill. Near the top of the hill was one wall of the Old City, and beyond that, Jerusalem. Down the hill from where the boys stood were ruins.

"Walk this way," the boys' teacher yelled so the class could hear. "Follow the guide." A thin woman near the teacher raised her hand so the kids could see her.

Everyone walked in a line down a narrow dirt path leading to the ruins. The ruins looked to Andrew like a pile of rocks. The way some rocks formed small walls reminded Andrew of his little sister's building blocks.

The path wound in and out of crumbling stone

walls. When the class finally stopped walking, they were inside the ruins and standing near a large pool of water. The pool was long and ran around another wall out of sight.

"This is known as Gihon (GIE-hun) Spring," announced the guide. "In ancient times, people in Jerusalem used tunnels to walk here. Just around this corner is one such tunnel." The teacher pointed to where the water disappeared around the corner.

"The people of Jerusalem used these tunnels in times of danger. When enemies approached the city, it was dangerous for people to leave the safety of the walls. But they needed the water, so they built tunnels. As you can tell by looking around, this spring is in a small valley. It is hard to see, even from a short distance. The ancient Israelites could sneak down that hill through these tunnels. They could reach this spring and get their water. Enemies never knew anyone left the city."

"How many tunnels are there?" one girl asked.

"There are several," the guide answered. "Some of them have collapsed, and you can't get through them anymore. Others are still in good shape. Now, if you will all follow me, we must go out that way." She motioned to the end of the room away from the pool.

As the class began moving out of the room, George stayed near the back of the group. "You guys go ahead," he told Andrew and Yoni. "I'm going to see where this pool leads."

"You could get in big trouble!" said Yoni.

"Let them try to stop me," George challenged.

As the last kids in the class left the area, George ducked around the corner. At first he didn't see anything special about the room. Then he saw an opening

leading into the ground. Boards blocked the entrance. He walked closer and peered through the cracks in the boards. He looked into the large hole and saw three or four small steps down. A path began at the bottom of the steps. It led into a dark tunnel. He pulled on the boards, but they would not budge.

George scanned the area for more tunnels and saw only one more. Broken rocks blocked it, and the opening was too small for him to squeeze through. He tried anyway. When he couldn't fit through the opening, he picked up one of the stones and threw it. He was going to clear a hole big enough to fit through if it killed him.

When the stone hit the wall near him, George noticed the funny sound it made. He looked where it had fallen and almost swallowed his gum. There were six blocks in the wall that were a little different color than the rest. He kicked the wall where the stone had hit, and it moved a little. He kicked three more times and finally pushed a block in enough to get his hand behind it. He peered inside and saw another tunnel leading from this place! It had to lead someplace important if it was hidden this well! George quickly took more stones from the first pile and hid the opening to the tunnel he had discovered. He ran to tell Yoni and Andrew what he had found!

It did not take long for him to catch up to the group. He quietly slipped in at the back of the class. No one noticed that he had been gone.

Chapter Five

On the bus back to the school, the boys talked excitedly.

"Think about it," George whispered. "Everyone needed water, even King David. A tunnel must have brought him water somehow. I mean, he was a king. He should have had indoor plumbing."

"But how are we going to find out where that tunnel goes?" asked Andrew.

"We'll go there this weekend," said George. "How about Saturday?"

"Can't," Yoni added. "Saturday is the Sabbath. Can you go Sunday?"

"Sure," George said. George and Yoni looked at Andrew.

"Do you think we really should go back there?" Andrew asked.

"You're kidding, right?" asked Yoni. "There's no telling where that tunnel leads."

"We HAVE to go back," George argued. "It's our DUTY. If there is a passage that no one knows about, it could lead someplace really important. Besides, it's not like it's restricted or anything."

"Shouldn't we just tell someone about it?" asked Andrew.

"No way!" Yoni answered. "If we tell someone, and it turns out there is something important down that tunnel, nobody will ever know we are the ones who found it. We found it fair and square. We have a right to be the ones to check it out."

"That's right," said George. "We could be responsible for finding something really important. We wouldn't get in trouble then. And if we don't find anything, we just won't ever tell anyone we were there."

"So what will it be?" asked Yoni. "Can you go back there with us Sunday after you get home from church?"

Andrew didn't answer Yoni right away. He thought about it for a long time. "George is right," Andrew thought. "We found the tunnel. It is only fair that we get the credit for it. And if we really do discover something important, nobody will care how we found it." After a while Andrew said, "Yeah, I can probably come Sunday."

"Yea!" the other boys cheered. "You won't be sorry."

Andrew hoped they were right.

✳ ✳ ✳

Time dragged before the weekend finally came. On Saturday, Andrew went with his dad to the market in Old Jerusalem again. It was quieter today because it was the Sabbath for the Jews. Many of them stayed home.

As he followed his father, Andrew thought about the next day. He smiled in excitement. The more he thought about it, the more excited he became. He didn't notice when his father stopped in front of the antique dealer's store.

"I forgot to pick up some bread for your mom," Andrew's dad said. "Can you wait here for me while I run back and get it?"

"Sure," Andrew mumbled, barely hearing what his dad said.

Andrew sat down on the steps leading into the antique shop. He didn't hear the footsteps creeping up behind him.

Chapter Six

Andrew sat deep in thought with his head in his hands. Suddenly a hand grabbed his shoulder. He gasped and jerked his head around.

"Hey, little hunter," a voice said.

Andrew looked up and saw the first antique dealer. He hadn't noticed where he was.

"Has your treasure hunting revealed anything important?" the man laughed.

"Not really," Andrew mumbled, looking for his dad down the street.

"No? But I thought you were going to be famous? Maybe you aren't looking in the right places."

Andrew knew the man was making fun of him. He wanted to tell him about the tunnel George had found. But he knew better than that.

"Do you have any more coins to show me?" the man asked. He reached for Andrew's pocket as if he was going to put his hand in it.

"Hey!" Andrew protested, pushing the man's hand away. "It's none of your business!" Anger swelled in Andrew. "I'll find plenty of important things. But you'll never see any of them. I know about secrets you only wish you knew! I know where there are secret tunnels. Almost nobody but me knows about them!" Andrew suddenly stopped. He knew he had said too much.

The antique dealer looked surprised. He bent low

and glared into Andrew's eyes. Their noses almost touched. The man's rotten breath floated past his yellow teeth. Andrew had to keep from gagging.

"It's not wise to know too many secrets," the man warned. "They have ways of getting you into trouble." He drew back and relaxed. "But I don't believe you. There are no more secret tunnels. Everything has been uncovered in the last 2,000 years. Do you think you could find something no one else has been able to find?"

The man paused and leaned down again. "But a young boy like you would be smart to stay away from secret passages, if there are any. They can be very dangerous places. You could disappear in one and never be seen again." With that, the man spun on his heel and went back into his store.

Andrew watched the man fade into the shadows of the store. "Andy! Over here!" Andrew turned to see his dad waving at him. "Come on down this way; I want to go back a couple blocks!" Andrew was happy to leave.

* * *

The next day, the boys crept into the ruins outside the wall of Old Jerusalem. It was only four o'clock in the afternoon, but the ruins were dark. The clouds and old walls blocked what little sun there was.

"It will take a little work to move the stones," said George. "But it shouldn't take us very long."

Andrew and Yoni saw the two tunnels George had told them about. Boards blocked one, and stones blocked the other.

"Over here," George motioned, "by this other

tunnel." He knelt down at the wall, near the tunnel blocked by rocks. "I put these stones here to cover the hole I made the other day." George moved the rocks. When Andrew saw the hole George had told about, his knees almost gave out.

"It's really true!" Andrew gasped.

"Cool!" said Yoni, dropping to his knees beside George to help clear the loose stones.

"This block should be easy to move," George said, as he pushed the first block in. "It's the one I moved the other day."

George put his arm into the hole and pulled on the other blocks around it. "I need help. These are really tight."

The boys worked for about 10 minutes to remove three more stones. "That's a pretty small hole," said Yoni.

"Yeah, but we can all make it through," George hoped.

Andrew lay on the ground with his head near the hole. "I'll squeeze through and help pull you guys in after me."

"Take this," George offered, holding out a flashlight. "It's probably pretty dark in there."

"I never would have thought of that," Yoni said, slapping his forehead with his hand.

Andrew snaked his head into the hole. Then he slowly slid his shoulders through. They scraped the rock and blocked the light. His eyes weren't adjusted to the darkness, but he inched forward anyway. The dark air smelled like his dad's shoes. He paused to wipe the cobwebs that tickled his face. Finally, he pulled his legs through the hole. Peering into the tunnel, he clicked on the flashlight.

Chapter Seven

"Wow," said Andrew from inside the tunnel. "This place is really big. When you get in here, you can stand up."

His flashlight beam bounced off the walls and ceiling. It was true that the boys could stand in the tunnel, but the ceiling wasn't as high as Andrew thought. Stones cluttered the path. Many had fallen from the ceiling, making it look higher than it was. The walls had been crumbling away for centuries. There was no telling what could happen if people began using the tunnel again. Andrew didn't notice how dangerous it looked. He was too excited about being in a secret passageway.

"Come on in," Andrew said. George had already started through the hole. Andrew grabbed his hands and helped him inside. Yoni didn't need any help. His skinny body slid through with ease. They brushed themselves off and checked the place out.

"Look at that," George whispered. He took the flashlight from Andrew. The light cut through the darkness several hundred feet ahead. At the end stood a wall where the tunnel turned out of sight. "Let's go!"

The boys moved as fast as they could through the rubble. They stopped as George turned the corner and shone the light ahead. The path ran a little ways and then split in different directions. Which way should

they go? George paused, afraid to keep going.

Andrew sensed that George was a little afraid. He held his hand out to George. "Let me see the flashlight. I'll go first."

George stiffened. He was afraid his friends thought he was chicken.

"You walked too fast with the light," Andrew smiled. "I couldn't see much. I'll walk slowly so you guys can see."

George acted disappointed. But he was glad Andrew wanted to lead the way. Andrew took the flashlight and stepped around the corner. He studied the paths and finally chose one. It wasn't very far before the tunnel turned uphill. It narrowed with each step.

"Hey," Yoni called quietly. "I think these rocks on the floor have fallen from the ceiling. This might not be a very safe place."

Andrew stopped walking and shined his flashlight around him. He noticed there were more rocks here than at the tunnel opening.

"Maybe we should go back," Yoni suggested.

"Nah, we'll be OK," George added, feeling safe because Andrew was in front. "Let's keep going. Maybe when we come to the next passage, we can try another tunnel."

Andrew continued up the tunnel and turned when the path split again. It was harder to walk because the tunnel grew steeper. "We must be going up the hill to the wall of Old Jerusalem," George decided.

"It sure would be easier to walk if we could stand up straight," Yoni added.

Andrew had not noticed that he was walking slower. All the boys were stooped over so they wouldn't hit their heads on the low ceiling. But they kept exploring. Sometimes Andrew led the boys down new tunnels. Other times they ran into dead ends and had to backtrack. After 30 minutes, Andrew suddenly stopped.

"Oomph!" George mumbled, running into Yoni. "Why did you stop?"

"Look," Andrew pointed. In front of him was a hole filled with water. It had a very small ledge on either side. It was nearly as big as the path was wide. "It looks like an old well," he guessed.

"Can we jump across?" Yoni asked.

"If we could stand up," said Andrew. "There's no way we can jump bent over like this."

"Can you creep along that ledge?" asked George, pointing to the small rim of the well.

"I think so," said Andrew.

The three boys carefully crept along the edge of the well like tightrope walkers. "I wonder how deep it is?" thought Yoni aloud.

"Beats me," said George.

The boys made it past the well and continued walking. A short time later, Andrew froze in his tracks.

"Listen!" he warned.

The boys stopped. They strained to hear.

"Voices!" said George.

"Are you sure those are voices?" asked Yoni. "They sound so far away."

"Listen to the echo," Andrew suggested. The boys listened for a moment, then the noise stopped.

"Which direction did they come from?" asked Yoni. Andrew pointed in front of them. But George pointed behind. The three looked at each other. There was no telling where the voices came from.

"Let's go back," said Yoni. The others agreed.

Andrew moved back down the path they had just come. He stopped at an intersection. "Did we come that way?" he asked.

George and Yoni shrugged. They were lost.

Chapter Eight

"Let's keep going the way we were heading," said Andrew. "This can't go much farther."

The boys walked a few more minutes. The ceiling was a little higher here. They could stand straight up as they walked. Occasionally the sound of voices grew louder.

"Great!" moaned Andrew. "A dead end!"

"Oh, man!" complained Yoni. "What are we going to do?"

"Look," said George, motioning to a spot in the ceiling. "There's a hole."

Andrew and Yoni looked up. Old boards blocked it off. But light trickled through the cracks.

"Give me a lift," Andrew said.

George and Yoni cupped their hands. Andrew stepped in them like a stirrup. He straightened and felt around the hole.

"These boards are really old," he said, picking at the wood. "Let's find a rock or something. I bet I can break through them."

In a moment, Andrew broke the boards. He cleared the hole and poked his head through.

"What do you see?" asked George.

"It's getting dark!" said Andrew. "How long have we been down here?" No one answered. "I see an alley. A cobblestone alley."

"Cobblestones?" asked Yoni. "We must be in Old Jerusalem."

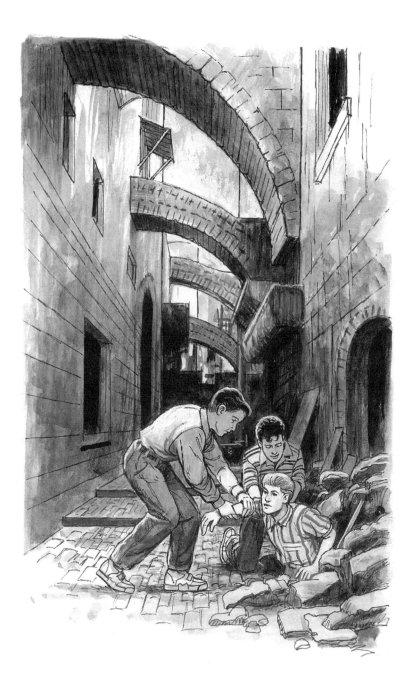

As Andrew looked around, he heard the voices again. "The voices are coming from out here. Help me get out."

George and Yoni lifted Andrew out of the hole. Because Yoni was the smallest, George boosted him up after Andrew. Then both boys pulled George up after them.

"Cover the hole," George said, grabbing a board lying in the alley. The other boys helped hide the hole.

"Where is this place?" asked George.

The sound started again, and Yoni spoke. "That's someone praying. It's a Hebrew prayer. We're in the Jewish quarter!" Yoni was relieved.

"Oh no!" moaned George.

Just then, loudspeakers sounded through the alley. It was like the sound of the Jewish prayer they were hearing, but it was louder and in a different language. George cheered. It was the call of the mosque (Islamic church), telling the Muslims to pray. The call sounded five times each day, and the boys all recognized the sound.

"It's OK!" smiled Andrew. "Jews are praying near Palestinian mosques. You guys are neighbors here!"

Somehow the thought didn't seem very comforting to Yoni or George.

The boys walked down two alleys, trying to figure out where they were in Old Jerusalem. After a minute, Andrew stopped. "Hey, I know where we are!"

"Where?" asked the others.

"Remember when my dad brought me to see the Dome of the Rock?"

Andrew was talking about a mosque. Inside the

building is a large rock. The rock is sacred to Jews and Muslims. Jews believe this was the rock on which Abraham nearly sacrificed Isaac. Muslims believe Muhammad stood on this rock before ascending to heaven.

"Well," continued Andrew, "this alley is near the back gates of the mosque! I hung out here while my dad was inside."

The boys raced down the alley and around the corner to see if Andrew was right. They saw a Jewish man in his prayer shawl. He sat next to the gates to the Dome of the Rock. The man was so deep in prayer he didn't hear the boys. Hoping not to disturb him, they quietly crept back into the alley.

The boys stood for a moment. The street grew darker. They were not sure what to do. Being in Old Jerusalem after dark can be pretty scary.

Chapter Nine

The boys ran. Crisscrossing streets and narrow alleys confused them. It was hard to tell where they were going. Andrew muttered something. But George and Yoni could not understand him. They were in too much of a hurry to get out of the alley. The dimming light made them slow down a little. Too many obstacles were hidden in the darkness. Finally they came to a large street. They stopped and looked around.

"This looks familiar," gasped Yoni, trying to catch his breath.

"Never been here before," Andrew sputtered. "Let's walk until we catch our breath."

After a few minutes, the boys came to one of the gates of the Old City. They recognized where they were. Andrew felt like a time traveler as he walked though the gates to the modern city of Jerusalem.

"We will need to catch a bus," George said. "We live too far from here to walk all the way home."

"Not I," countered Yoni. "We are pretty close to my house. I'll see you later." He dodged around a corner and out of sight. George and Andrew listened as Yoni's footsteps faded.

"There's the bus stop," said George, pointing across the street.

"I wish I knew what time it was," Andrew said.

Soon the bus pulled in front of George and Andrew. They quickly took their seats. "Why were you talking to yourself back there when we were running?" asked George. His head jerked as the bus moved down the rough street.

"What? Oh, I was just thinking, 'Do not fear. Do not fear.' Was I saying that aloud?"

"Yeah," laughed George, "you were talking to yourself."

"Just a verse I learned in Isaiah."

"Huh?" George didn't understand.

"You know," said Andrew, "in the Bible—the Book of Isaiah. Chapter 41, verse 10 says, 'Do not fear, for I am with you.' I remembered it when we ran. It was pretty scary back there."

✽ ✽ ✽

The next day was Monday. At school the boys talked about the previous day's event.

"It was pretty cool," said George, "but I don't think I want to go back there again."

"Not in a hundred years," vowed Yoni. "There is no telling what was in those tunnels. And there were so many passageways you could get lost forever."

"I'm so glad we finally found that hole by the mosque," said Andrew. "I don't know how we ever could have found our way out if it wasn't for that."

George and Yoni soon forgot about trying to find any more treasure. But Andrew didn't.

✽ ✽ ✽

Thursday afternoon Andrew walked into his house after school.

"Hey, buddy," Mr. Anderson said, peeking out from behind his newspaper.

"Hey, Dad," Andrew smiled. "Why are you home so early?"

Mr. Anderson pointed to the front page of his newspaper. "I figured today would be a good day to stay home and relax. I don't get many chances to take a day off."

Andrew looked at the newspaper and wrinkled his forehead. At first he thought his dad had pointed to a sports story. But then he saw the headline: "TUNNEL SYSTEM FOUND UNDER TEMPLE MOUNT: POLICE SUSPECT UNAUTHORIZED EXCAVATIONS!" Andrew almost lost his breath. Mr. Anderson read the article aloud:

> Three unidentified men were caught by soldiers near the Temple Mount last night. The men are charged with unauthorized excavating in the tunnels below the Mount. The soldiers said they are careful to note strange activity in the area. The men were found in a restricted area. The area has been closed to archaeologists for more than 80 years. It is sacred to both Palestinians and Jews. The army refuses to release the identities of the men in order to avoid political or religious demonstrations. They have placed armed guards at the sight. Old Jerusalem is now under a 10 P.M. curfew.

As his dad read, Andrew sat down. Were these the same tunnels he had been in earlier that week? He knew the news story had nothing to do with him, but he was worried.

"What's wrong, Andrew?" Mr. Anderson asked.

"Huh?"

"You look white as chalk."

"What's this all about?" Andrew asked.

Mr. Anderson explained. "Remember when we went to see the Dome of the Rock?"

"Yeah."

"Temple Mount is that whole area of Old Jerusalem. It is where King Solomon built the original Temple. That area is the most holy place in the world for Jews. For Muslims it is the third holiest site. The Jews agreed not to violate the Temple Mount by digging. In return, the Muslims allow the Jews to worship peacefully at the Western Wall, called the Wailing Wall. The Jews know there aren't many ruins left from the old Temple. But they would love to find anything that may still be there. This has been a problem for many years."

Andrew didn't say anything. He ran to call Yoni.

"Did you read the paper?"

"Yeah!" said Yoni. "Do you think they will find us?"

"No. I think these guys were in one of the other tunnels we passed. My dad said they caught people going in to dig up stuff. That definitely wasn't us!"

"Then who was it? This is getting scary. The Temple is the most holy place for Jews. This could cause big problems around here."

"No kidding."

"What should we do?" asked Yoni.

"I don't know. I really want to find out what's going on. Maybe we can find a signet ring there after all."

"Yeah, and end up dead or in jail," added Yoni.

"Come on. It's not that bad. If we could only get back inside that tunnel . . . ," said Andrew. "I'm going to call George."

Andrew hung up the phone and dialed George's number. George answered.

"George, have you seen the paper today?"

"Yeah!" George announced. "I was just trying to call you. My dad thinks there may be riots tomorrow!"

"Really? Riots?"

"The Muslims are very angry," said George. "They say the Jews weren't protecting the holy place."

"What about the curfew? Did you hear about that?" asked Andrew.

"Oh, what's up with that? The Jews goof up, and the Palestinians have to pay for it."

"They don't know if it was a Jew or not," Andrew said. "It could have been anyone."

"Whoever it was has caused some big problems," George said.

"I want to go back," Andrew told George.

"But—"

"We won't do any digging. But if the tunnels go near the Temple, think of what we could find!"

"It would be really cool," confessed George. "How would we do it?"

"Instead of going in at the entrance in the City of David, we could go in through the alley. Remember where we came out last time?"

"Do you think they've found that hole yet?" asked George.

"I don't know. We could always try. It will be hard to convince Yoni to go with us, though."

Chapter Ten

Andrew and his friends walked through the streets and alleys of Old Jerusalem. Nighttime was falling. They figured it would be easier to get back in the tunnels after dark. Yoni was against the idea of going into the tunnels again. But George convinced him that all the activity proved it contained lost treasures.

"There sure are a lot of people out tonight," Yoni said quietly.

"Yeah," said George, "and they are forming groups."

"Is that bad?" Andrew asked.

"When crowds of Palestinians and Jews meet, it's usually very bad," said George.

Andrew started muttering. George heard what he was saying this time: "'Do not fear, for I am with you, do not be afraid, for I am your God'" (NRSV).

The boys hurried to the Dome of the Rock and down the alley where the tunnel exited.

"It's open!" Andrew said. "No guards!"

The three ran to the tunnel opening near the ground and moved the boards. Andrew dropped through the hole. Yoni and George followed.

Inside the tunnel, all three clicked on flashlights.

"Where to?" asked Yoni.

"This way." Andrew led the group. When he found another passageway, they turned. Andrew wanted to take a different route than last time.

After only a few minutes, the tunnel became larger. All three boys could stand straight. They walked until the tunnel opened into a large room with a dirt floor. Yoni shone his flashlight straight up to the ceiling high above.

"What is this place?" George asked.

"Who would build something like this underground?" asked Andrew.

"Look!" said Yoni. At the far end of the room was a stone archway, leading into darkness.

The boys moved to the other end of the room. What they saw almost made them drop their lights. The archway led into a huge chamber. It was twice as big as the room they had just left. Scattered around the room were rickety tables made of boxes and wooden planks. On the tables sat ancient pots and oil lamps, glassware and old coins. On the largest table sat a golden menorah. A menorah (me-NOR-ah) is a Jewish candleholder that holds seven candles. But this menorah was broken and had only three candleholders left. The floor of the room was littered with shovels and buckets and piles of dirt.

"What are these things?" Andrew asked.

"Relics from the Temple!" Yoni said, amazed. His mouth hung open. "All this must have come from the ancient Temple," he explained.

George spoke up, "It was probably put here before the Temple was destroyed."

"Someone's been digging here." Andrew pointed to the buckets and shovels.

"Oh, man, it's those people from the newspaper. The ones they caught!" panicked Yoni.

"They must not have caught all of them," George added.

"Wait!" Andrew motioned for the others to be quiet.

"Footsteps!" George whispered. "Lights off!" The others clicked off their flashlights. They scrambled behind a row of boxes.

In seconds the room filled with light. Andrew guessed by the brightness that the person carried a lantern. The boys breathed as quietly as they could. They heard the person shuffling around the room. The light stopped moving. The boys heard nothing. Andrew thought the person might have left.

The boys' legs cramped as they waited. Yoni shifted and blindly touched the ground. His hand hit something small and metallic. He picked it up to look at it but was interrupted by Andrew. Andrew turned to whisper to George and Yoni but froze and stared over their shoulders. Yoni and George followed his gaze. A man stood with his back to them. He backed slowly toward the boys while he read something in his hands. The boys grabbed each other for balance. They wanted to run but knew the man would hear. Andrew imagined the others could hear his heart thumping. Suddenly, the man spun around and nearly tripped over the hiding boys.

"Ahhh!" cried the man. "You!"

It was the antique dealer from Old Jerusalem! Andrew tried to run, but his feet felt like cement. The boys could only stare, afraid of what might happen next.

"Ha! I see you've stumbled on your great find, my boys," the man said. His dark beard shook as he laughed. "And in such a short time." The man waited for the boys to respond, then continued. "So how did you find this place? Did I say something to give it

away?" The dealer suddenly growled, "Or was it dumb luck?"

"It was just an accident," Andrew managed to whisper hoarsely.

"Hmmm," the dealer thought. "I can understand that. I, too, found this place quite by accident."

The boys didn't say a word.

"Imagine my surprise as I walked home from prayers one evening," the man said. "I stumbled over a pile of stones in an alley. And there I found an entrance to this tunnel. No doubt you know exactly the place I mean. My friends and I began digging here, and look what treasure we found. They were arrested. But the police think everyone was caught. What you see here is all mine!"

Andrew's fear turned to anger when he realized the man meant to steal the treasures.

"But I really wish you hadn't found my secret place. If you boys tell anyone, you will destroy the prize of my life. There will also be riots—maybe even war." The man's voice sounded threatening.

The boys gulped. Yoni managed to say, "War?"

"Yes, the Muslims will be outraged to know what we have done. And the Jews will stop at nothing to continue the search. So you see, no one must find out what we have discovered. I cannot let you leave."

The boys sat frozen. The man eyed them as he stroked his beard. It occurred to George that the man had no way of making them stay. He had no weapon. And they had to be faster than he.

"Too bad," George finally said. "Run!" Yoni and Andrew wasted no time following George's order. They bolted out of the room and into the tunnel. The man followed closely behind. He reached and grabbed Andrew's shirt. But Andrew jerked and tore away. The pursuit continued until the tunnel grew smaller. The man had to almost crawl. The boys gained a lot of distance. Soon they stood under the opening to the alley. They wasted no time getting out the way they had before. Yoni and George boosted Andrew up through the opening.

Before Andrew could look around outside, a large stone struck the ground near the opening to the tunnel. Yoni came up through the hole and gasped. The boys had escaped the man only to find themselves in the middle of a riot!

Chapter Eleven

"Look out!" Andrew yelled, as Yoni crouched beside the hole. More rocks landed near them.

"Oh, man!" Yoni yelled. "Hurry, George!"

George crawled out of the hole, and the boys scrambled into a nearby doorway. All around them Palestinians yelled and threw things. Standing on the stairs in the doorway, the boys could see down the street where Israeli soldiers stood. Behind the soldiers, a yellow ribbon blocked an entrance similar to the one the boys had found, only bigger.

The crowd was very angry. Young men and women hurled rocks and bottles toward the soldiers. They yelled curses at the soldiers for allowing the Temple area to be invaded. A few Jewish men in the crowd also yelled at the soldiers. Here and there Palestinians and Jews fought one another. The boys watched a Jewish teenager swing a broom handle at a Palestinian man who held a broken bottle. Both were bleeding. But the crowd just let them fight. Andrew said over and over, "'Do not fear, for I am with you. Do not fear, for I am with you.'"

"We've got to run for it!" George said, pointing back down the alley.

"No way!" Yoni yelled. "We'll get killed!"

"If we stay here, we'll probably get killed too!" Andrew said.

"Yeah, but if anyone notices I'm Jewish, I'm finished for sure!"

"Look, Yoni, I'll yell that I am Arabic so the crowd won't turn on us," offered George.

"As we run, you duck and I will cover your head," Andrew said. It hadn't occurred to Andrew that he might be mistaken for a Jew as he protected Yoni.

"I don't know," Yoni thought aloud.

"Please, Yoni!" George begged. "We've got to get out of here!"

"OK. Let's go," Yoni decided.

As they left the protection of the doorway, George yelled, "I am Arabic! I mean no harm!" Yoni and Andrew yelled, too, hoping it would keep the crowd from hurting them. The crowd was too loud. Nobody heard the boys as they headed down the alley. But three teenagers saw the boys trying to escape. Thinking they must be Jewish, the teens threw a brick and some rocks at Andrew. Andrew fell, grabbing the back of his head. George and Yoni pulled on Andrew's arms.

"Get up! They're coming."

Andrew's mind grew cloudy. His eyes would not focus. And his legs felt like noodles. But he knew he had to get away. Andrew ran as Yoni and George held on to his arms.

"He's bleeding!" Yoni screamed.

George pulled his shirt off and held it against the back of Andrew's head.

"Ah, forget 'em," said the teenager who threw the brick. "That'll teach them not to come back here."

The boys escaped out the other end of the alley. They ran down the street. As they rounded a corner, all three of them ran into a group of Israeli soldiers heading toward the riot. Falling to the ground, one soldier grabbed a club hanging on his belt. He yelled at the boys, thinking they were part of the riot. He raised his club, but another soldier grabbed his arm.

"Stop!" he ordered. "Who are you?"

"We are trying to get away from the riot," said Yoni in Hebrew. "We accidentally got stuck in the middle of it. My friend was hit in the head. He's bleeding pretty bad. We have to get him to a doctor."

George kept pressure on Andrew's head. Andrew's mind became clearer. But his head hurt worse than he could imagine. The pain made it hard for him to think.

The soldier spoke into his walkie-talkie. "Unit Six. Leader here. We have a child injured in the riot. We need an ambulance immediately!"

"Sit right here," he told the boys. "An ambulance will be here soon. If you leave, you may find yourself in another mess." The soldiers ran off in the direction of the riot.

"'Do not fear . . . ,'" Andrew mumbled. He couldn't remember the rest.

"'Do not fear, for I am with you,'" reminded George.

"What's that?" Yoni asked.

"Just something Andrew says all the time," George said. "I don't really know what it means."

In a very short time, an ambulance arrived. It took the boys to a hospital outside Old Jerusalem. Andrew was quickly taken into an examining room.

"Do you boys know how to reach his parents?" the doctor asked George and Yoni.

"Yes, sir."

"Go have the nurse call them. This boy is going to stay with us for a while."

* * *

By the time Andrew's parents got to the hospital, he had 15 stitches in his head.

"Oh, honey, are you all right?" Mrs. Anderson cried, grabbing her son.

"Yeah, Mom, I'm fine," said Andrew. He looked at his friends, and his face turned red. But it felt good to hug her.

"How did all this happen?" Andrew's father asked.

"He'll have to tell you that later," the doctor interrupted. "Your son has a concussion. It's only a small bruise on his brain. But I'd feel better if we kept him here tonight."

"Of course," said Mr. Anderson, "whatever you think is best."

Yoni and George left to call their parents. When they returned to Andrew's room, the boys told Andrew's parents everything that had happened.

Andrew's parents remained quiet during most of the story. Mrs. Anderson couldn't help adding an "Oh my!" now and then. And they did not look pleased when George told of how he found the tunnels.

"So George and Yoni helped me get away from the riot. That's when we met the soldiers. And that's who called the ambulance," Andrew finished.

Andrew's parents were quiet for a long time. Finally Mrs. Anderson spoke up.

"Didn't you realize what you were doing was wrong?"

"We never thought it was wrong," said Andrew. "The tunnel wasn't restricted. There were no signs saying to keep away."

"What about when the newspaper said the tunnels were being guarded?" asked Mr. Anderson.

"We knew it was dangerous. But we weren't going to steal anything," Yoni said. "We just wanted to find something from the past."

"Even if it meant trespassing in a holy area," said a voice from the doorway.

Everyone turned to see George's parents standing just inside the room.

"Boys, don't you understand what it means when a place is sacred?" said Mr. Abu-Hannah. "We must respect holy objects and places. You showed no respect by your actions."

The boys began to see what they had done was wrong. They argued a little, but they knew the truth.

"I'm just glad you're all safe now," Mrs. Anderson said, hugging Andrew again.

Another voice came from the hallway. "This is his room."

Yoni's mom and dad knocked on the doorframe and entered. When they saw George's parents, they stopped. Mr. and Mrs. Abu-Hannah looked angry and nervous.

"We'll wait out here until you're finished," said Yoni's parents, backing out of the room.

"Never mind," said George's mom coldly. "We were just leaving. Come on, George."

Everybody was quiet and tense. George and Yoni's parents didn't like each other much because of religious differences. The recent events in Old Jerusalem made it worse.

"Mom, can Yoni and I talk to Andrew privately?" George asked. "It will only take a minute."

George's mother and father looked at each other.

"OK," said his dad. "We'll be in the waiting room."

The adults left the room, and the boys were alone.

"Wow, that was weird," said Andrew. "I never realized your parents didn't like each other."

"They've never met before," said Yoni.

"I don't understand it," said George to Yoni. "We're best friends. But people think we should hate each other."

"No," said Andrew, "you're supposed to love each other. We're all supposed to love each other. The Bible says God is love. Jesus showed us how to love everyone. Hate is something people tell you to do."

"You really believe in that Jesus stuff, don't you?" George asked.

"He's more than a prophet," said Andrew. "He's God's Son."

"If anyone else told me that," added Yoni, "it wouldn't mean anything to me. But you mean it. You aren't perfect, but you always try to do what's right."

"Even though he gets into trouble too!" George laughed.

"It's Jesus in my life that helps me do what's right," said Andrew. He looked at George. "Even though I don't always make the right choices! But God takes care of me as I learn to do what He wants me to do."

"Is that what that verse is all about? That one you've been saying all the time?" asked George.

"'Do not fear, for I am with you, do not be afraid, for I am your God,'" said Andrew. "I learned that during the Gulf War. Remember when our church sent us to Cyprus during that war? My dad taught me that. It's hard to be brave sometimes, so I like to remember that verse. It helps me when I am afraid."

"I thought the Bible was just for you to preach to non-Christians," said George.

"No. It helps Christians too. God speaks to us in what the Bible says. It's good for a lot of things."

George and Yoni thought about what Andrew said. Finally George said, "I gotta go. My folks are waiting for me. But I think I'm going to have a lot of questions for you about your Bible."

"Bring it on!" Andrew laughed.

"We'll see you later," Yoni waved. "I better be going too."

"I think he's faking it," George joked to Yoni as the two left.

"Yeah," said Yoni, putting his hands in his pockets. "Those stitches are probably fake!"

* * *

Out in the waiting room, the parents wondered what was taking their boys so long. Mrs. Anderson worried about Andrew's head, and a Bible verse came to mind.

"'Don't be afraid; just believe,'" she said quietly (Mark 5:36).

"Did you say something?" George's mother asked.

"As a matter of fact, I did," said Mrs. Anderson. Silently praying for courage, she began to talk about Jesus.

* * *

As the two boys walked back to the waiting room, Yoni pulled something out of his pocket.

"What's this?" he thought. Then he remembered.

"Hey, George, look at this. I found this when we were hiding from that old man. In all the excitement, I forgot about it."

"What is it?" asked George. Both boys stopped and looked at the round metal object.

"It looks like a coin," said Yoni. "And it's got a Star of David!"

"Maybe it's from a signet!" said George.

"Andrew! Hey, Andrew!" yelled the boys, running back down the hallway toward their buddy's room.